RUSSIAN SLANGUAGE

A *FUN* VISUAL GUIDE TO RUSSIAN TERMS AND PHRASES BY MIKE ELLIS

DEDICATED TO SUZANNE, VIRGINIA, MIKEY, AND PHIDGETTE

First Edition
21 20 19 18 17   5 4 3 2 1

Text © 2017 Mike Ellis
Illustrations © 2017 Rupert Bottenberg, except illustrations of yeti on page 6 © 2017 Reno Martin/Shutterstock.com; knot on pages 9, 11, 37, 38, 41, 43, 44, 63 © 2017 Wiktoria Pawlak/Shutterstock.com; skull on pages 9, 39 © 2017 Tribalium/Shutterstock.com; duck on pages 9, 12 © 2017 Cattallina/Shutterstock.com; bowl on pages 22, 24, 25 © 2017 vectorisland/Shutterstock.com; foot on pages 24, 25 © 2017 IhorZigor/Shutterstock.com; seat on pages 30, 89 © 2017 Double Brain/Shutterstock.com; nut on pages 32, 71 © 2017 Aleks Melnik/Shutterstock.com; pole on pages 34, 63, 88, 90 © 2017 totallypic/Shutterstock.com; peace sign on page 48 © 2017 Gl0ck/Shutterstock.com; gnome on pages 56, 64 © 2017 Alena Rib/Shutterstock.com; pie on page 69 © 2017 Brian Goff/Shutterstock.com; cup on page 78 © 2017 iconizer/Shutterstock.com; peach on page 81 © 2017 Kalenik Hanna/Shutterstock.com

Published by
Gibbs Smith
P.O. Box 667
Layton, Utah 84041

1.800.835.4993 orders
www.gibbs-smith.com

Designed by michelvrana.com

Gibbs Smith books are printed on paper produced from sustainable PEFC-certified forest/controlled wood source. Learn more at www.pefc.org. Printed and bound in Hong Kong

Library of Congress Cataloging-in-Publication Data

Names: Ellis, Mike, 1961- author.
Title: Russian slanguage / Mike Ellis.
Description: First edition. | Layton, Utah : Published by Gibbs Smith, 2017.
Identifiers: LCCN 2016039990 | ISBN 9781423646815 (pbk.)
Subjects: LCSH: Russian language–Glossaries, vocabularies, etc.--English.
Classification: LCC PG2640 .E46 2017 | DDC 491.783/421–dc23
LC record available at https://lccn.loc.gov/2016039990
ISBN: 978-1-4236-4681-5

CONTENTS

HOW TO USE THIS BOOK

If you have always wanted to learn the basics of Russian, but traditional methods seemed overwhelming or intimidating, this is the book for you! Just follow the directions below and soon you'll be able to say dozens of words and phrases in Russian.

• Follow the illustrated prompts and practice saying the phrase quickly and smoothly.

• Emphasize the words or syllables highlighted in red.

• A strikethrough means you don't pronounce that letter or letters.

• Learn to string together words or phrases to create many more phrases.

• Draw your own pictures to help with memorization and pronunciation.

Note: This book may produce Americanized Russian.

For free sound bytes, visit slanguage.com.

GREETINGS AND RESPONSES

Hi
Привет
Privet

Pre Vee Yeti

How are you?
Как ты?
Kak ty?

Cocktail?

Good afternoon
Добрый день
Dobryiy den'

Doe Bray Dean

Good evening
Добрый вечер
Dobryiy vecher

Doe Bray Vee Chair

Good night
Спокойной ночи
Spokoynoy nochi

Spa Coy Neigh No

Sheet

Good-bye
До свидания
Do svidaniya

Dust Vee Don Ya

Bye
Пока
Poka

Pa Cod

Congratulations
Поздравляю
Pozdravlyayu

Post Rough Lay You

Excuse me
Извините
Izvinite

Ease Vee Neat Yuek

Go away
Уходи
Ukhodi

Moo Cut Dee

I don't understand
Не понимаю
Ne ponimayu

Knee Penny My You

You are beautiful
Ты прекрасна
Ty prekrasna

Tee Pre Cross Knot

How much?
Сколько?
Skol'ko?

Skull Car?

Please/You're welcome
Пожалуйста
Pozhaluysta

Pa Jowls Duck

In my opinion
По-моему
Po-moyemu

Poe Moy Moo

Just a moment Минутку *Minutku*	**Me Newt Cool**
Mr. Господин *Gospodin*	**Ghost Buy Dean**
Mrs. Госпожа *Gospozha*	**Gus Pa Shop**
Last name Фамилия *Familiya*	**Fam Meal Yet**

Yes
Да
Da

Dot

Knee Yet

No
Нет
Net

Talk See Bee Yet

Not too well
Так себе
Tak sebe

Lad Knot

Okay
Ладно
Ladno

Sit down
Садитесь
Sadites'

Welcome
Добро пожаловать
Dobro pozhalovat'

What time is it?
Который час?
Kotory chas?

Sad Deed Tees

Duck Bro Pa Shallow

It's

Cot Oh Ray Chess?

FAMILY AND FRIENDS

Mother
Мать
Mat'

Mutt

Brother
Брат
Brat

Brat

Daughter
Дочь
Doch'

Deutsche

Son
Сын
Syn

Sin

Grandmother Бабушка *Babushka*	**Bob Bush Cod**
Couple Пара *Para*	**Pod Ah**
Person Человек *Chelovek*	**Chill Levee Ick**
Guest Гость *Gost'*	**Ghost**

FASHION

Blouse
Блузка
Bluzka

Blues Car

Boots
Ботинки
Botinki

But Team Key

Bracelet
Браслет
Braslet

Brass Let

Coat
Пальто
Pal'to

Pal Toe

Gloves
Перчатки
Perchatki

Pants
Брюки
Bryuki

Pocket
Карман
Karman

Ring
Кольцо
Kol'tso

Pear Chat Key

Brew Key

Car Mondo

Called Sew

Shoes Туфли *Tufli*	**2 Flea**
Shorts Шорты *Shorty*	**Shore Tay**
Sneakers Кроссовки *Krossovki*	**Cross Off Key**
Socks Носки *Noski*	**Nuss Key**

Sweater
Джемпер
Dzhemper

Tuxedo
Смокинг
Smoking

Stylish
Стильный
Stil'nyiy

To iron
Гладить
Gladit'

James Pear

Smoking

Steal Knee

Glide It

SPORTS AND ENTERTAINMENT

Author
Автор
Avtor

After

Basketball
Баскетбол
Basketbol

Basket Bowl

Bell
Колокол
Kolokol

Coal Oh Coal

Boxing
Бокс
Boks

Box

Chess
Шахматы
Shakhmaty

Shock Ma Tay

Cinema
Кинотеатр
Kinoteatr

Kin No Tee Art Up

Clown
Клоун
Kloun

Clone

Gymnastics
Гимнастика
Gimnastika

Gimme Nasty Car

Football
Американский футбол
Amerikanskiy futbol

Am Eddie Con Ski

Foot Bowl

Hockey
Хоккей
Khokkey

High Key

Horse racing
Скачки
Skachki

Scotch Key

Movie
Кино
Kino

Key No

Rugby
Регби
Regbi

Rag Bee

Soccer
Футбол
Futbol

Foot Bowl

Tennis
Теннис
Tennis

Ten Niece

VERBS

To be hungry
Быть голодным
Byt' golodnym

Bite Gal Load Numb

Vee Bee Rat

To choose
Выбирать
Vybirat'

To do/To make
Делать
Delat'

Deal It

To release
Отпускать
Otpuskat'

Ought Poo Scat

To remember
Помнить
Pomnit'

Pom Neat

To rescue
Спасать
Spasat'

Spa Sat

To sit
Сидеть
Sidet'

Seed Eat

To smell
Пахнуть
Pakhnut'

Pock Newt

To speak
Говорить
Govorit'

Govern Eat

To steal
Красть
Krast'

Crest

To surround
Окружать
Okruzhat'

Ah Crew Jet

To take
Брать
Brat'

Bright

To understand
Понимать
Ponimat'

Pony Mott

Nice Seat

To wear
Носить
Nosit'

Pea Sat

To write
Писать
Pisat'

ADJECTIVES AND ADVERBS

Absolutely
Абсолютно
Absolyutno

Ab Soul Loot Nut

Poe Sleep

After
После
Posle

Again
Снова
Snova

Snow Va

At night
Ночью
Noch'yu

No Chew

Before
Перед
Pered

Period

Calm
Спокойный
Spokoynyiy

Spa Coy Knee

Dangerous
Опасный
Opasnyiy

Up Puss Knee

Dirty
Грязный
Gryaznyiy

Grass Knee

Dishonest
Нечестный
Nechestnyiy

Knee She Yes Knee

Empty
Пустой
Pustoy

Poos Toy

Full
Полный
Polnyiy

Pole Knee

Honest
Честный
Chestnyiy

Chest Knee

In addition to В дополнение *V dopolneniye*	**Voodoo Paul Niña**

In front of Спереди *Speredi*	**Spear Eat Tee**

Inside Внутри *Vnutri*	**V'New Tree**

Inside out Наизнанку *Naiznanku*	**Neighs Non Coo**

Last
Последний
Posledniy

Paws Lee Knee

More
Больше
Bol'she

Boy Shut

Near
Около
Okolo

Oh Cola

Nice
Приятный
Priyatnyiy

Pre Yacht Knee

Occasionally
Порой
Poroy

Pod Up We

Old
Старый
Stariy

Starry

On top of
На вершине
Na vershine

Knot Very Sheeny

Personally
Лично
Lichno

Leash Knot

Poor
Бедный
Bednyiy

Quickly
Быстро
Bystro

Realistic
Реалистичный
Realistichnyiy

Recently
Недавно
Nedavno

Bee Yet Neigh

Boy Straw

Realist Teach Knee

Need Of Knot

Silent
Тихий
Tikhiy

Slippery
Скользкий
Skol'zkiy

Smooth
Гладкий
Gladkiy

Soon
Скоро
Skoro

Tee He

Skulls Key

Glad Key

Score Up

Still Еще *Yeshche*	**Ye Show**

Strong Сильный *Sil'nyy*	**Seal Knee**
Tidy Аккуратный *Akkuratnyiy*	**Ah Coo Rot Knee**
Under Под *Pod*	**Put**

Useful
Полезный
Poleznyiy

Poe Lee Yes Knee

Usually
Обычно
Obychno

Ah Beach Knot

Weak
Слабый
Slabyiy

Slobby

Wide
Широкий
Shirokiy

Shared Oh Key

PRONOUNS, PREPOSITIONS, AND CONJUNCTIONS

About
Примерно
Primerno

Although
Хотя
Khotya

And
И
I

But
Но
Ho

Pre Me Air Knot

Cut Yet

E

No

Each/Everybody
Каждый
Kazhdyiy

Cars Dee

He
Он
On

Own

I
Я
Ya

Yet

Knot

On
На
Na

They
Они
Oni

To
До
Do

We
Мы
My

While
Пока
Poka

Honey

Doe

My

Pock Car

BUSINESS AND LABOR

Accountant
Бухгалтер
Bukhgalter

Book All Tier

Accounting
Бухгалтерия
Bukhgalteriya

Book All Tee Dee Yacht

Business
Бизнес
Biznes

Bees Nest

Carpenter
Плотник
Plotnik

Plot Nick

Desk
Стол
Stol

Stole

Kiosk
Киоск
Kiosk

Key Owes'k

Letter
Письмо
Pis'mo

Peace Moe

(Computer) Mouse
Мышь
Mysh'

M'Wish

Order
Порядок
Poryadok

Pod Yacht Dock

To pay
Платить
Platit'

Plaque Teat

Physicist
Физик
Fizik

Fee Zeke

Pilot
Пилот
Pilot

Pea Lot

Soldier
Солдат
Soldat

Store
Магазин
Magazin

● Soul Dot

Magazine

HEALTH AND MEDICINE

Are you okay?
Вы в порядке?
Vy v poryadke?

Viv Buy Yacht Key?

I need a doctor
Мне нужен доктор
Mne nuzhen doktor

Mini Up Noodgin' Doctor

I cut myself
Я порезался
Ya porezalsya

Yet Putty Salsa

Bandage Повязка *Povyazka*	**Poy Vee Ask Up**
Bath Ванна *Vanna*	**Vonn Up**
Cold Простуда *Prostuda*	**Prop Stewed Ah**
Height Рост *Rost*	**Roast**

Infection
Инфекция
Infektsiya

To scratch
Чесать
Chesat'

In Fee Yeck Sun

Cheese Sat

EDUCATION

Angle
Угол
Ugol

Google

Astronomy
Астрономия
Astronomiya

Astra Gnome Me Up

Biology
Биология
Biologiya

Bee Ah Low Key Up

Chalk
Мел
Mel

Meal

Chalkboard
Доска
Doska

Desk Cod

Chapter
Глава
Glava

Glove Up

To divide
Делить
Delit'

Delete

Eraser
Ластик
Lastik

Lie Stick

Experiment Эксперимент *Eksperiment*	**Ex Speedy Meant**
File folder Папка *Papka*	**Pop Cod**
History История *Istoriya*	**His Story Yacht**
List Список *Spisok*	**Speed Suck**

Mathematics
Математика
Matematika

Matt Tee Monty Cod

Paper clip
Скрепка
Skrepka

Scrape Cod

Pencil
Карандаш
Karandash

Cod On Dash

Projector
Проектор
Proyektor

Pry Hector

Psychology Психология *Psikhologiya*	**Seek Up Low Key Up**
Radius Радиус *Radius*	**Roddy Owes**
School Школа *Shkola*	**Sh'Cola**
Semester Семестр *Semestr*	 **See Me Esther**

Sheet of paper
Лист бумаги
List bumagi

Least Boo Ma Key

Sum
Сумма
Summa

Assume Up

Symbol
Символ
Simvol

Seem Volt

System
Система
Sistema

See Stem Up

NUMBERS AND TIME

Day
День
Den'

Dean

Year
Год
God

Goad

Noon
Полдень
Polden'

Pole Dean

Spring
Весна
Vesna

Visa Knot

Fall Осень *Osen'*	**Oh Sin**
Number Номер *Nomer*	**Gnome Air**
One Один *Odin*	**Ah Dean**
Two Два *Dva*	**D'Vah**

Three
Три
Tri

Tree

Ten
Десять
Desyat'

Day Sit

Twenty
Двадцать
Dvadtsat'

D'Vah Sit

Hundred
Сто
Sto

Stow

Million
Миллион
Million

Me Lee Own

Billion
Миллиард
Milliard

Me Lee Yard

TRANSPORTATION AND TRAVEL

Airplane
Самолет
Samolet

Sam Eye Load

Airport
Аэропорт
Aeroport

Ida Port

Avenue
Авеню
Avenyu

Avenue

Car
Машина
Mashina

Mush Sheen Up

Corner
Угол
Ugol

Google

To cross
Пересекать
Peresekat'

P.D. See Cuts

Flight
Полет
Polet

Pie Gloat

Ship
Корабль
Korabl'

Cod Ah Bull

Steering wheel
Руль
Rul'

Rule

Subway
Метрополитен
Metropoliten

Metro Poll Lee Ten

Taxi
Такси
Taksi

Tack See

Ticket
Билет
Bilet

Bee Lee Yet

Tire
Шина
Shina

Sure Nut

Tourist
Турист
Turist

2'd East

Train
Поезд
Poyezd

Poised

Wheel
Колесо
Koleso

Collie Sew

FOOD AND
RESTAURANTS

To eat
Есть
Yest'

Yeast

Eye Bee Yet Debt

To have lunch
Обедать
Obedat'

Yet But Car Teal . . .

I would like . . .
Я бы хотел . . .
Ya by khotel . . .

Moo Tee Buy Yeast . . . ?

Do you have . . . ?
У тебя есть . . . ?
U tebya yest' . . . ?

Bottle
Бутылка
Butylka

Boot Teal Cod

Check
Чек
Chek

Check

Drink
Напиток
Napitok

Nap Pea Took

Fork
Вилка
Vilka

Veal Cod

Sip
Глоток
Glotok

Glad Toke

Paul Neigh Wrote

Mouthful
Полный рот
Polnyiy rot

Slice
Ломтик
Lomtik

Loam Tick

Pod Nose

Tray
Поднос
Podnos

Restroom
Туалет
Tualet

2 Wally Yet

Lunch/Dinner
Обед
Obed

Eye Bee Yet

Sweet
Сладкий
Sladkiy

Slot Key

Sour
Кслый
Kislyiy

Kiss Lee

Delicious Вкусно *Vkusno*	**V'Coo Snot**
Yum-yum Ням-ням *Nyam-nyam*	**Knee Yum Knee Yum**
Yuck Тьфу *T'fu*	**T'Food**
Apple Яблоко *Yabloko*	**Yab Low Cod**

Banana
Банан
Banan

Banana

Beer
Пиво
Pivo

Pea Va

Broccoli
Брокколи
Brokkoli

Bro Cup Lee

Carrot
Морковь
Morkov'

More Cough

Cheese Сыр *Syr*	**Sear**
Chicken Курица *Kuritsa*	**Coo'd Eat Sock**
Chocolate Шоколад *Shokolad*	**Shook Ah Lot**
Cocoa Какао *Kakao*	**Cake Cow**

Date	**Fee Nick**
Финик	
Finik	

Y'Eat Sew

Egg	
Яйцо	
Yajtso	

Car Toe Fell Free

French fries	
Картофель фри	
Kartofel' fri	

Cheese Knock

Garlic	
Чеснок	
Chesnok	

Ice
Лед
Led

Load

Lemon
Лимон
Limon

Lee Moan

Peach On Cod

Liver
Печенка
Pechenka

Lollipop
Леденец
Ledenets

Lee Den Knee Yets

Mango Манго *Mango*	**Manga**
Onion Лук *Luk*	**Luke**
Peach Персик *Persik*	**Pear Seek**
Persimmon Хурма *Khurma*	**Core Ma**

Pie
Пирог
Pirog

Pea Rug

Plum
Слива
Sliva

Sleeve Ah

Potato
Картофель
Kartofel'

Car Toe Fell

Radish
Редька
Red'ka

Reed Cod

Salt
Соль
Sol'

Soul

Sandwich
Бутерброд
Buterbrod

Boo Tier Bro'd

Sausage
Колбаса
Kolbasa

Coal Bus Up

Sugar
Сахар
Sakhar

Sack Her

Tea
Чай
Chay

Chaise

Trout
Форель
Forel'

Far Ale

HOUSEHOLD

Address
Адрес
Adres

Balcony
Балкон
Balkon

Cable
Кабель
Kabel'

Chair
Стул
Stul

Address

Ball Cone

Car Bell

Stool

Dressing table
Туалетный столик
Tualetnyiy stolik

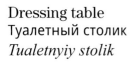

Toilet Knee Stole Lick

Floor
Пол
Pol

Pole

House
Дом
Dom

Dome

Kettle
Чайник
Chaynik

China Nick

Laundry
Стирка
Stirka

Match
Спичка
Spichka

Metal
Металл
Metall

To paint
Красить
Krasit'

Steer Cod

Speech Cod

Me Towel

Cry Seat

Pole Cod

Shelf
Полка
Polka

Par

Steam
Пар
Par

Stole

Table
Стол
Stol

NATURE AND WEATHER

Branch
Ветка
Vetka

Vee Yet Cod

Chestnut
Каштан
Kashtan

Cash Ton

Coast
Берег
Bereg

Bee Dig

Crocodile
Крокодил
Krokodil

Crock Ideal

Fir
Ель
Yel'

Yell

Fog
Туман
Tuman

2 Money

Forest
Лес
Les

Lee Yes

It's windy
Ветренно
Vetreno

Vee Yet Rain No

Planet
Планета
Planeta

Plan Yet Ah

Reptile
Рептилия
Reptiliya

Rep Tee Lee Yet

River
Река
Reka

Reek Cod

Sand
Песок
Pesok

Pea Soak

Smoke
Дым
Dym

Deem

Stem
Стебель
Stebel'

Steer Bill

Tulip
Тюльпан
Tyul'pan

Tool Pond

Violet
Фиалка
Fialka

Fee All Cod

RUSSIANGLISH

The words listed below have the same meaning and essentially the same pronunciation in both English and Russian. Although you may experience small slanguage pronunciation differences, you will still be understood.

- Airport
- Bar
- Brunette
- Budget
- Café
- nter
- mpion
- eur

- Chocolate
- Class
- Computer
- Director
- Hockey
- Humor
- Hurrah
- Internet

- Jeans
- Jihad
- Journalist
- Menu
- Number
- Parachute
- Passport
- President

- Robot
- Rocker
- Sex
- Student
- Telephone
- Video
- Vodka
- Zebra